Eliminate Negative Thinking

A Guide To Overcoming Negative Thoughts And Doubt – Declutter Your Mind And Shift To Positive Thinking, Self-Love, And Mental Strength

DERICK P. ALLAN

Contents

Introduction

In today's world, more and more people are suffering from negativity and anxiety. It is getting increasingly difficult to function, and while medicine is making great strides, a great number of people find themselves incapacitated and drowning in fear and negativity.

If you feel like you can't cope with the day to day struggle and if you're doubting your own capabilities, you are not on your own. Anxiety is rife and our current way of living, which often leads to isolation and high levels of stress, makes many of us feel lonely and powerless.

A lot of people find that they cannot reach out to others when they are struggling with mental problems. This is often due to ongoing stigmas, which still exist even though they are slowly decreasing. People are afraid of appearing weak, so everyone struggles on alone, without asking for help when they need it.

Almost every single person in the world will have struggled, at some time or another, with doubts and anxieties. Almost everyone will have thought 'I am not good enough' or 'I cannot do this' at some point in their lives. Negativity is a powerful force, and it's something we all get subjected to at times.

However, you don't have to let it rule your life. You can fight against it and empower yourself. You can eliminate the negativity and reduce your anxiety, and we are going to show you how. In this book, you'll delve into the concept of negativity, and come to understand why it is such a prevalent force in so many people's lives.

We'll then uncover some top strategies for fighting back and changing your life, exchanging negativity for positivity, and minimising stress. With these techniques, you can take back control and revolutionise your way of thinking. This is about taking charge, adjusting your approach, and empowering yourself so that you can live positively.

CHAPTER ONE

What Causes Negativity?

If you are feeling negative and struggling with aspects of your life, the first thing you should do is to try and trace this negativity back to its roots. Why are you feeling low? What is creating this sensation and what can you do about it?

Let's look at the different kinds of negativity.

Negativity With A Cause & Negativity Without A Cause

Sometimes, there will be an obvious cause, but often, you'll be suffering from anxiety or negativity for no clear reason whatsoever.

Either situation can be difficult to deal with, but in many ways, not having a root cause that explains the anxiety can be worse. Let's look at why. There are three top reasons.

☐ Firstly, if you know that you are upset about a specific thing, it is easier to rationalise that eventually, this thing will pass and the negativity will go with it. This isn't a 'fix all' solution to painful life events, but it can help to put them into perspective and make it easier to deal with them.

However, if you're stuck with no obvious cause for the negativity, you might feel like you're going to be suffering from it for years, possibly for your whole life. If you don't have an obvious cause, it's much harder to get a sense of when it will end – and you might even feel like it will never end. If nothing is triggering it, there is nothing to stop triggering it, after all.

☐ Secondly, you may feel more frustrated with yourself if you are struggling with negativity without a clear cause. You might be thinking things like 'My life is good. I am extremely lucky because X, Y, Z. What's wrong with me? Why can't I be happy?'

Often, this will make the feelings of negativity worse, because you start to blame yourself and get angry with yourself. Your frustration doesn't have another source to focus upon, and it may end up turning inward, which will only increase the negativity and start you on a path of self-hatred. Obviously, this needs to be addressed.

☐ Thirdly, it is hard to take action to reverse the negativity if it has no clear trigger. If you know that you are upset because of a bad breakup, you can make efforts to spend time with friends and focus on your well-being. If you know that you are down because you have lost someone, you can find ways to bring

ELIMINATE NEGATIVE THINKING

positivity to their memory and inject happiness into your life. These techniques won't always work, but being able to take some action usually makes people feel better.

However, when your negativity has no clear cause, it's hard to find 'counters' that let you work against it and help you to overcome it. There are still things you can do, but it may be much harder to identify them in instances where you don't know what's making you feel low.

You might be wondering why we feel negative if there is no apparent reason for it. How is this a useful survival strategy?

Why Do We Feel Sad?

There is a whole range of things that might cause you to feel sad, and in this section, we'll cover some of those that are harder to pinpoint. Don't worry if none of these feel like they apply to your situation; there are so many things that can have an impact on your thoughts and feelings, and these are just a few. There may be other things that are making you feel unhappy which aren't listed here.

Physical Issues

Sometimes, feelings of sadness can be a result of something physical. For example, if you haven't slept or you

• 11 •

are starting to go down with an illness, the negative physical feelings (which you may not even have noticed yet) can have a major impact on your mood, making you feel low, irritable, angry, or frustrated. The physical symptoms can be very mild and still translate into your mood.

Many people joke about 'getting out of bed on the wrong side' as an explanation for this. It relates to an old superstition that says putting your left foot down first when you're getting up leads to a bad day. While the superstition may sound crazy, it demonstrates that a somewhat inexplicable bad mood can follow us from the moment we get out of bed.

This is probably linked with poor sleep more often than we realise. You may have had a good night, but if you're catching up on lost sleep from another night, this can make you feel surprisingly badly rested, and annoyed with the world as a consequence.

Equally, a slight headache, a sore throat, physical pain, or just a general sense of unwellness – even one that you have not consciously noticed yourself – can contribute to feelings of negativity.

The great thing about physical issues being the root cause is that on the whole, they will pass off with time, and you should find that the negative mood lifts, leaving you feeling much better. However, if you have got yourself into a 'habit' of feeling low, that may not happen even when the cause (the physical feeling) has disappeared. Let's look at this next.

Patterns Of Negativity

It is unfortunately very simple to 'train' our brains into feeling bad. Don't be angry with yourself if you think that this has happened, because it is all too easy to do. We all depend on habits, because they make our lives easy, but sometimes we slip into negative habits, and these can be very hard to break. If you've trained your brain to habitually respond with negativity in most situations, you're going to have to work to un-train it.

The more negative your internal dialogue is from day to day, the more your brain will learn these sensations. Brains repeat what they know and it can be amazingly difficult to change a wrong belief, so if you have fallen into a patch of negativity for other reasons, you might find that it is extremely difficult to drag yourself out of it, because your brain has learned the bad feeling.

You will then habitually turn towards this feeling at every moment. If you have ever checked your wrist for a watch you aren't wearing anymore or tried to pick up your phone when it's already in your hand, you'll know how powerful habits are, and they can work on your emotions just as they can on your actions.

If your habitual response to a situation is negative, this will become a vicious cycle that constantly brings your mood down and makes everything worse, which makes your habitual response even more negative. You have taught your brain to expect something bad, and this is – to an extent – a self-fulfilling situation, because it will be more aware of bad things, and keener to log them to confirm its own bias.

Negative habits are extremely hard to break, but it can be done with work. We will talk about this later, but for now, think about whether your negative responses have become habits. If someone says something ambiguous to you, do you automatically assume the worst? Do you get anxious when planning an event because of all the things that might go wrong? Do you spend hours thinking about disasters that will probably never happen? This is all habitual negative thinking, and it needs to be addressed.

Blue-Coloured Glasses

You have probably heard the phrase 'rose-coloured glasses.' This indicates that the person is looking at everything in the best possible (and unrealistic) light, and may be easily misled. They are choosing to tint the world to fit with their beliefs. We all do this to an extent, but often, we're unaware of just how much our mood colours our perception of events. We think we are dealing with them objectively, but actually, our approach can vary massively from day to day.

It is surprising, in a way, that there is no alternative phrase to the rose-coloured glasses for negativity. We view rose-coloured glasses, even though they are associated with a positive outlook, as a bad thing, because they hamper our ability to deal with fact and logic. The same goes for blue-coloured glasses, through which everything feels negative.

Thinking about the kind of figurative glasses you put on in the morning can be really helpful. We are usually very unaware of how we are colouring every moment of our lives with perspective, but heightening your awareness may help you to counteract the colour – whether it's red or blue – to a degree, because you will know it is there, and you can account for it. You might still reach for the blue glasses in the morning, but at least you will know you are wearing them.

If you need an example of this, try to think about a bad day at work. You could probably list a myriad of tiny problems that built up to make it really challenging, alongside some bigger issues.

If you objectively compared this day with what you consider a good day, you would likely find there is a lot more overlap in the two than you think. It's just that on a bad day, minor inconveniences stack up and seem more problematic than they are, whereas on a good day, you dismiss them or don't even notice them.

Even something as simple as dropping your pencil can seem earth-shattering when you are having a bad day. On a good day, you would probably barely register it falling. You could pick it up and move on without a second thought, while bad-day-you stared at it in fury and despair, wondering why you are so incompetent as to not even manage holding a pencil properly.

Remember: perspective really matters.

Hormones

It's easy to dismiss hormones as something that we should have left behind as teenagers, but they can have a massive impact on your mood, and they are very hard to identify. How do you know if your body is releasing more oxytocin today than it was yesterday? How do you know if your serotonin levels are high?

Women may be more aware of hormonal imbalances than men, because menstruation often causes more noticeable and serious fluctuations and can lead to low mood or elation. Similarly, pregnancy can have an impact. However, hormones can affect the mood of either sex, and men should not dismiss the power that hormones have over their sense of happiness and well-being.

Even things like the time of year can have an impact upon your mood, because our bodies respond differently to long hours of darkness and low amounts of sunlight. You may find that you struggle more with negativity during the winter, especially in the long stint after Christmas, when spring has not yet arrived and the cold season seems to be dragging on indefinitely.

Although hormones have a massive impact on a person's mood, remember that they don't control you, and it is possible to do things about hormonal imbalances. A doctor may be able to help if there is an issue that you are struggling to deal with alone. Depression as a result of hormones can come and go, but taking medication that regulates your hormones will help you through the more difficult moments.

Mental Disorders

It's very easy to end up trapped in a cycle of negativity because of a mental disorder, and huge swathes of the population suffer from such disorders. Depression, seasonal affective disorder, bipolar disorder, persistent depressive disorder, and many other mental problems can make you feel low at seemingly random times. You could be 'on top of the world' in many ways – with a loving family, a great job, a secure home, and plenty of luxuries – and still feel negative about everything due to one of these disorders.

Anyone can suffer from a mental disorder, regardless of what they have experienced in life. The stigmas surrounding such problems are beginning to dissolve, but many people still feel 'weak' or powerless in the face of admitting that they suffer from them.

It is important to be honest with yourself about mental issues and your relationship with them, because it is almost impossible to overcome a mental disorder through sheer willpower and positive thinking. Some of the strategies that we cover later in this book may help you to combat mental problems, but you should still take a proactive approach and discuss them with a doctor to ensure that you are getting the help you need.

Often, the most powerful attack on a mental disorder is two-pronged, and requires both intervention from a medical professional and exercises in positivity from you. Going for only one approach and neglecting the other is a far less effective way to combat issues with negativity.

This section is not a conclusive list of all the things that can cause negative thinking, but it should help to give you some idea about what may be at the heart of the issue when there is no obvious reason for a low mood. Many other things could also be contributing, but don't assume that there is 'no reason' to feel sad and get frustrated with yourself just because you can't pinpoint the cause of the negativity. The brain is far more complicated than we often give it credit for, and even the top scientists don't yet have a full understanding of how things can impact on our moods and sense of the world.

In the next chapter, we're going to look at why negative feelings make such a significant difference to our lives and why we need to deal with patterns of negativity before they become too ingrained. After that, we'll move on to looking at the things you can do about negativity and how to get yourself out of the rut.

CHAPTER TWO

Why Does Feeling
Negative Matter?

The obvious answer to this question is: it matters because we don't like to feel sad. Sadness is seen as something to be avoided at all costs, and if you are feeling low, you usually try to do anything that you can to change the emotion and make yourself feel better.

This is true regardless of what has made you feel bad, or whether you can pinpoint the source of the negativity. Nobody likes to have a 'low day,' and there are quite a few negative emotions associated with it, as well as sadness. Feeling negative matters because it changes how we behave and at times stops us from having a positive impact upon the world. Few of us feel proud of how we act when we are feeling down in some way.

Anger, frustration, aggression, selfishness, etc., all tend to stem from feeling negative or unpleasant. It's important to acknowledge that feeling down twists our sense of fair play and can make it harder for us to care about other people and their feelings at times. Many people do use sorrow to do something good for the world, of course, but it's key to remember how powerfully negativity can affect how we interact with other people and events in our lives.

We touched on this in the previous chapter, but let's expand more fully here to express just how powerful negativity is over every aspect of your life.

Scenario one:

Kate has just got up to go to work. She is feeling good and looking forward to the day, so she starts hunting around for her clothes. Her socks have somehow ended up under the desk, flung there while kicking off her clothes for bed last night, which makes her chuckle as she picks them up. The coffee winds up on the floor when she's trying to pour it – whoops, but it's early and she's sleepy and these things happen.

She has soon got the mess cleaned up and she's off to work, leaving at 7:45 as usual. She gets held up in traffic and ends up a few minutes late, but it's no big deal and she soon settles in for her day.

Scenario two:

Kate has just got up to go to work, and she's feeling low. She doesn't want to go in, and she already knows it's going to be a bad day. The missing socks confirm it, and she starts to curse herself for not putting them somewhere sensible, and wondering why she can't be like 'normal' people who fold their clothes up at night. If she had just done that, she'd already be eating breakfast, and she wouldn't have to rush. What sort of stupid person doesn't put their socks where they can find them?

Kate rushes downstairs to make a coffee, but the water slops over the edge of the mug and she mentally berates herself for her clumsiness. Now she has to clean up, as well as work a long day, and if she hadn't been so careless, everything would be easier.

Kate still manages to get out of the door for 7:45, but the traffic is bad and she's late for work, and it's all her fault for being disorganised and a poor planner, because she should definitely have left earlier and built more time into her schedule, even though the events were beyond her control. Everyone is probably staring at her and wondering what sort of adult can't get herself to work on time.

You can probably see how in the second scenario, the small things like looking for a pair of socks and spilling some water get blown out of proportion and become a focal point for blame even though they are minor inconveniences that would be far less of an issue if Kate didn't feel like they were an issue. Her stress magnifies the problems which, in the first scenario, are barely registered and just considered a normal part of life. Everything is seen in a negative light.

The negativity drives a need to blame someone. Something bad has happened, and someone must be at fault for that. Some people will blame their friends, strangers, their significant other, their kids, or even their pets, because they want an outlet to drive the negativity into; it feels good. If you've ever shouted 'stupid computer' at a totally inanimate object that can't hear you and has no concept of the insult anyway, you'll understand this desire to lash out. In itself, this act of lashing out is hurtful and unproductive, but it also leads to a secondary problem.

Most of the time, even if they blame others for these events, people will blame themselves too. They will look for a fault in themselves, even as they are telling somebody else they have done something wrong, and often this self-criticism is subconscious but very strong. 'You're so stupid, you can't even pour a cup of coffee.' We've probably all done this on particularly bad days, and it sounds borderline ridiculous if you stop and examine it, because what does intelligence have to do with being able to pour coffee, and since when is that a measure for self-worth?

No matter how illogical it is, many people do allow negativity to affect them in such ways. The missing socks become a reason to berate yourself and call yourself names for not doing something you 'should' have done. The missing socks are evidence of all your failings – whereas on a good day, they are nothing more than an extra thirty seconds you spend while getting dressed, and they have no further significance than perhaps a flicker of amusement as you finally spot them.

This isn't to say that you should never study your behaviour and seek to improve it when you cause yourself difficulties. Observing a fact such as 'I always leave too late and end up stressed at work' is a useful means of improving your life, because you can take action to change the issue. Think of it like a performance review at work, where you learn how you can do something better.

However, the observations and conclusions we draw when stressed and feeling negative are rarely so lucid, and almost never productive. Observe the language that Kate used about herself. She did not focus on a solution to the problem, e.g. putting the socks with the rest of her clothes, but on her own failings to be 'normal.'

Such observations aren't designed to instigate change. They are just critical, without looking for improvement. Their only purpose is to satisfy the negativity by driving it into something. Why does this feel good? It's hard to say – why do we want to punch something when angry? Why do we feel grimly satisfied when the villain gets their comeuppance? It just feels good.

Kate's sock incident could – at a stretch – result in self-improvement, because she is observing a behaviour that has caused her an issue and, if she then thinks about this rationally and without the negativity, she can make an effort to put her socks somewhere else in the future. However, she then goes on to blame herself for a small coordination slip and for traffic that she had no control over, because she needs something to project the negativity onto, and she chooses herself. Rational or irrational, she uses herself as an outlet for frustrations.

It is extraordinary how prevalent this behaviour is in many societies, and most people are unaware that they are doing it. How often have you called yourself a name because you said something out of place or unintentionally upset someone? How often have you thought of yourself as lacking because of something perfectly normal that you did which didn't turn out as well as you'd hoped?

Everyone does this to varying degrees and in small doses, introspection and self-observation can help us, but many people take it much too far. They are not thinking rationally about self improvement, but instead irrationally attack themselves for 'flaws' because it satisfies the negative sensation.

If you only do this occasionally, it is probably not very important in the grand scheme of things. If you've once mentally told yourself off for spilling coffee, it doesn't really matter. Kate's single bad morning is not a huge issue if it stays a rare occurrence.

However, one of the problems with this kind of negativity is that humans fall into habits very easily, and laying blame is something that we love to do. If you make yourself a target for blame too regularly, you will start to do this in every negative moment, and find yourself at fault for anything, no matter how irrational the blame is.

Obviously, this will feed into feelings of anxiety and heighten your negativity. If someone is standing at your shoulder every minute of every day and telling you that you've just done X wrong, you are bound to believe them eventually – even if that someone is just a voice in your own head. The more anxious you get, the less capable you will be of dealing with things, which will further fuel your self-doubt and your tendency to blame yourself when something goes wrong.

The more ingrained this habit of self-blame becomes, the harder it will be to notice it, and the more you will do it. You may also start to project the blame onto others around you more and more, partly from a desire to defend yourself from your own accusations, and partly just due to the habit of needing to blame any bad occurrence on something or someone.

Overall, then, feeling negative a lot of the time can have a massive impact on your life because you will seek to express that negativity through blame, and often that blame will turn inwards. In turn, that will breed more negativity, feeding into a vicious cycle where you are at fault for everything, and everything is bad. You will never focus on finding solutions or improving the situation, but just on working out where the fault lies.

It's very hard to break these cycles. Habits become deeply ingrained and often so instinctive that they are difficult to even notice. However, it can be done, and in the next chapter, we are going to look at how you can take control of your negativity and stop laying blame on yourself and on others.

This will make you more resilient when it comes to dealing with problems, because you won't also be grappling with guilt and anger when something goes wrong – and you will look for solutions, rather than seeking to find someone who is at fault.

CHAPTER THREE

Physical Exercise

So, we have looked at what causes negativity and why it's so important to recognise and deal with it, and now it's time to discuss some strategies for addressing low mood and unhappiness. You may not be surprised to see that physical exercise is at the top of the list of things to do when you aren't feeling good – and yes, it is also very hard to commit and do it when you aren't feeling good.

It has been consistently proven, however, that exercising is one of the ultimate ways to change your mood. When you work out, your body releases endorphins that make you feel better, and there is no arguing with this. It may not always work, or it may not be sufficient to pull you out of a rut, but it is nonetheless a massively important aspect of keeping your mood high and making you feel good.

There are a number of reasons for this besides just the temporary release of endorphins that occurs when you work out.

The first of these is the sense of accomplishment. When you don't feel like you have achieved anything much in a day, that sense of disappointment will feed into your negative dialogue and increase its ammunition for saying you don't do enough and you aren't giving it your all. While you want to address that at its root and stop measuring yourself in this way, it can be useful to also have ways of proving the voice wrong. Giving yourself the achievement of exercising is one such way.

If you get up early and head to the gym or go for a run, you are immediately achieving something with your day, and giving yourself a sense of worth because you have done something that many people in society aspire to do. You are also taking the time to care for yourself, and putting time and effort into your physical well-being.

Psychologically, this transfers a sense of worthiness to you; you are valuable enough to look after and put time into. You are important enough to care for.

The effect is therefore double-pronged. Not only can you applaud yourself for making the effort to exercise, but you have reminded yourself of your intrinsic and immutable value as a person. This can be a powerful combination, and one of the fastest and perhaps easiest ways to boost your mood and make yourself feel good.

Exercising is also a great way to give yourself a sense of power. You don't have to gain muscle or lose weight for this to take effect; just the act of doing something physical is often enough to remind you that you are in control and you have agency.

There is a small danger, however, that exercise will become a further stick to beat yourself with if you aren't careful. You must not allow yourself to slip into the habit of berating yourself when you fail to get to the gym or go for a run. Life happens, and nobody can manage this at all times, so don't trap yourself by making exercise a rigid part of your routine and feeling devastated when you can't achieve it because other things get in the way.

However, do take the time to exercise when you can. Saying 'no' to other commitments and making space for you and your bodily well-being is another way to convey value onto yourself and adjust your priorities to ensure that you feel like you matter. Don't shrink your exercise routine to fit in with what other people want or need and then feel disappointed in yourself for not managing to workout. This is definitely counter-productive.

Making exercise part of your routine is a good way to get around this. Rather than going to the gym erratically, when you have time, try to build about ten to twenty minutes of exercise into your daily routine, or at least weekly routine. This will help you to stick at it and make it a normal part of life for you.

Remember, you don't have to take up running, weightlifting, or other intense exercises if you don't want to or you feel uncomfortable with that. Exercise can be following a dance video on YouTube, learning karate, going for a swim, or playing tennis with friends. You do not need to be on a treadmill in the gym or lapping marathon runners. You just need to be having fun and moving your muscles.

Let's look at some of the top tips for getting into the habit of exercising.

Tip One: Exercise With Friends

It may sound obvious, but the more you can enjoy exercising, the easier it will be to do. Some people feel like exercise needs to be exhausting and punishing to be worthwhile, and that if it's too enjoyable, it can't be as good for you.

That isn't the case, of course. You can get a great workout just running around with a ball and your friends, and you are much more likely to get involved with this sort of thing because it's more fun. You can also benefit from spending some quality with your friends, so even if you don't want to make group exercise your regular go-to option, it's worth considering for an occasional mood lifter.

You never know which of your friends might also benefit from this sort of activity, so do try this out. It will boost your mood and their moods, as well as improve the physical fitness of everyone involved. Just make sure you don't choose friends who are ultra competitive, as this might spoil the game. Keep it light-hearted and fun, and it will go much better.

If you would rather not do big group exercising or this just isn't feasible with your schedule, consider finding a running buddy (or just a gym buddy). You don't need to get together every time, but it's great to have someone to bounce ideas off, motivate, and be motivated by. This makes exercising a far more engaging aspect of life, and something to look forward to, rather than a chore to despise.

Tip Two: Do Something You Love

Try out as many different kinds of exercise as you can until you find something that really makes your heart sing. All kinds of exercise can be good for you, so try dancing, cycling, running, hiking, walking, skipping, martial arts, Pilates, yoga, tai chi, aerobics, swimming, squash, tennis, basketball, or any other team sports.

There are so many things that you can do, so make sure you try as many different sports as possible, and see which suits you. Remember, there is no 'right' way to exercise, so whatever feels good and makes your heart sing is right for you. You shouldn't feel you have to stay tied to one sport over another just because you have been a lifelong swimmer. If it's no longer bringing you joy, try something new out.

This has the added benefit of working out different muscle groups and avoiding strain on certain body parts. You will get more benefits from varied exercise than from one rigid go-to option.

Tip Three: Try Cold Water Swimming

An increasing number of studies are being done on the effects of cold water on the mood. The exhilarating shock of diving into ice cold water seems to be a surprising mood boost for many people, and it is thought that this could help combat depression and anxiety.

An early example of this sort of science includes the Open Water Swimming As A Treatment For Major Depressive Disorder,[1] which found that swimming in freezing open water led to a reduction in the need for medication in the person undertaking the trial. This was followed by a complete halt in taking any medication, and the effects of this continued into the follow up the next year.

Obviously, this is a single case and it is not advised that you drop medication just because you take up cold water swimming, but if you are interested in boosting your mood, you may find it useful. If you have access to an area where you could take up cold water swimming, you should definitely give this a shot.

Tip Four: Take Rest Days

It is always important to take days off when it comes to exercising. This is true no matter how athletic you are. It has

1   van Tulleken C, Tipton M, Massey H, et al Open water swimming as a treatment for major depressive disorder Case Reports 2018;2018:bcr-2018-225007.

been consistently proven that rest days make your exercise more valuable, and they are an opportunity to cut yourself a bit of slack and be kind to yourself.

Remember, it is crucial not to turn exercise into a weapon that you use against yourself in a flow of negative thinking. If exercise only becomes a source of guilt because you aren't doing it, it isn't helping to reduce the flow of negativity.

There will be days that you don't make your goals. There will be days when you don't get to the gym (or squash court, swimming pool, or path around your house). The only way in which this matters is how you respond to these events and what they mean in terms of your positive journey. Do not allow them to become problems. Nobody makes their fitness goals a hundred per cent of the time; it is okay to take it easy sometimes.

It is also important to take it easy from a physical perspective. Rest days improve your ability to exercise well in the following days, allowing your muscles to heal. They reduce the risk of injury and often help you to progress towards your fitness goals faster.

Make sure you set some days in your exercise routine where you don't feel obliged to work out. Taking a break is another way of conveying value to yourself, rewarding yourself, and improving your mental well-being.

Remember, exercise is a very valuable tool in the fight against negativity and anxiety. Use it both when you are feeling low and when you are feeling good. It will make you feel better both physically and mentally, and is often a major aspect of recovering from negativity.

Mood Boosting Activities

As well as physical health, it's crucial to look at your mental health. There are many mental exercises you can undertake that will improve your mood and make you feel better. You can interrupt negative thinking with some conscious positivity, but it takes work, so in this chapter, we are going to explore some top tips for doing it.

Tip One: A Positive Mental Dialogue

We have discussed how a negative mental dialogue can be extremely detrimental and take over your whole life, so let's now look at the power of a positive mental dialogue, and how you can use this against the negativity.

You may already have heard of positive affirmations and self-empowering language, and you may even have tried to use them. Unfortunately, for many people, this is very challenging. It is far easier to criticise ourselves than it is to praise ourselves, partly because most modern societies teach us to be humble and modest.

Sometimes, self-criticism is also a defensive mechanism; if we criticise ourselves, it stops others from doing it, because we have beaten them to the punch. Often, the criticism we anticipate is not there, but by putting ourselves down, we feel safer.

Take a moment to pause and think about your mental dialogue. How do you talk to yourself? What things do you say to yourself when something goes right? What things do you say to yourself when something goes wrong? Do you ever call yourself names?

It's worth making a list of the things that you commonly tell yourself, whether aloud or in your head. Becoming aware of these things is the first step to challenging negative thoughts, because half the time, you may not even hear yourself say them otherwise.

Some phrases you may be familiar with include:

☐ You're so stupid

☐ That was dumb

☐ Why are you overreacting?

☐ You can do better

☐ That isn't good enough

☐ You're clumsy

☐ Other people are ahead of you

☐ Nobody likes you

☐ Why would you do that?

☐ You shouldn't talk to people

☐ You should be able to do this by now

☐ You aren't clever

☐ That was immature

☐ You're being selfish

☐ This should be easy

☐ Don't be an idiot

Obviously, these will vary from person to person and you may find that your negative thoughts are completely different to those listed here, but spend a bit of time trying to identify them. Whenever you find a new negative thought that you fall back on, write it down.

Listen to your internal dialogue and try to 'snapshot' your instant reaction when something goes wrong so you can determine whether or not you are being unfair to yourself.

You should write down things even if they don't seem wrong, or they are positive. This should give you a good picture of how you view yourself and what areas you are struggling with. Make note of how you approach a situation where you have excelled, and how you approach a situation where something has gone awry (whether or not it is your error).

When you have a comprehensive list, sit down and examine it, and make some observations about your overall attitude and go-to responses. Decide whether they are positive or negative overall, and think about which phrases you would like to change.

Tip Two: Would You Say It To A Friend?

Once you have identified some of your common phrases and the way in which you talk to yourself, it's a good idea to think about whether that is okay.

Take each of your common phrases and ask yourself whether you would say it to a friend or a stranger. If you wouldn't say it to a friend, why is it okay to say it to yourself? Are you not your friend? Wouldn't life be pleasanter and easier if you were?

Secondly, ask whether you would be hurt if someone else said it to you. If your partner or your best friend or one of your children said such a thing, would you be upset?

Next, if you overheard someone say it to somebody else, what would you think about the two people involved? Would you think one was harsh and critical? Would you think the other was genuinely stupid or deserving of the criticism, or is there another way that the criticising person could have framed their comment that would have been more useful?

Taking this sort of perspective on your internal dialogue can make it much easier to see when you are being unfair to yourself. We are often much harder on ourselves than we are on other people, and thinking about saying one of your common phrases to a stranger can really help you to see how damaging it might be.

Tip Three: Is It Useful?

Next, assess your critical thoughts in terms of usefulness. How helpful is the internal commentary? What does it do for you?

Take, for example, the comment 'You can do better.' In theory, you might think that this comment is helpful to you because it encourages you to do and be more than you already are, and to strive for improvement. In reality, however, it is not helpful, and here's why:

The phrase 'You can do better' has no context and does not offer any concrete improvement opportunity. It is an arbitrary judgement that doesn't consider either the amount of effort that you put in or the difficulty of the challenge. It also doesn't explore *how* you can do better, which is really the crucial information here.

If you have this thought, pull yourself up on it and instead of stopping there, decide why you think you can do better and how you can do better.

Let's begin with the why. What stopped you from doing well the first time? Were you at a disadvantage? If it's a new activity or you misunderstood an instruction then yes, this thought might actually be useful and can serve as motivation to have another go. If, however, you just think this whenever you do something and weigh up the final result, you aren't gaining anything but negativity.

This leads us to the how factor. How could you do better? Here is the key part of the thought process. What would you change next time?

Let's look at an example.

Scenario one:

Tom has just finished a work project and handed it in. His boss is satisfied with it and gives it the go-ahead, but when Tom gets the material back, he thinks 'I can do better.' The project has been approved and there's no reason for him to do anything else, so Tom tosses it aside, moving on to the next project.

He retains nothing but a slight sense of dissatisfaction, and when the next project rolls around, he starts with a sense of negativity about his general ability to perform well when it comes to such projects. The scenario repeats, because he does not take the time to question the negative thought, and he doesn't attempt to funnel the criticism into anything useful.

Tom has not gained anything but negativity with this 'I can do better' thought. He has not considered what went wrong, or how he could do better. He has not analysed his weaknesses or any difficulties presented by the working environment.

When he next comes to a project, he cannot either approach it from a better position or do things differently. He is liable to repeat the same mistakes, and if the negative thinking turns into a pattern that doesn't lead to any improvement, Tom's work will start to suffer because he will consistently believe he isn't doing his best, but is taking no steps to improve.

Scenario two:

Tom gets his work project back and sits to review it. He reads over what he has done and notes that early on in the project, he made a mistake. He didn't gather all the information he needed, which meant he had to go back and redo early parts of the project. While he corrected the error, this meant he couldn't put much time into polishing the finished piece, and it wasn't as good as he wanted it to be by the time it was handed in.

When Tom's next project rolls around, he makes a greater effort to collate all the information he needs before he gets going, giving himself more time at the end for making the project shine.

In this case, Tom still knows that something went wrong, but instead of leaving it as a vague notion of dissatisfaction, he delves deeper. He looks at what he did wrong – not getting the information he needed – and works out what to do next time instead. The focus is shifted from the 'wrong' onto the 'next time,' and the negativity is turned into an empowering action that takes the focus off the bad feeling.

This is not an easy habit to form, but it is a good one. When you have a negative thought, ask yourself whether it is a useful negative thought. If not, dismiss it. If you can use the thought, focus on the usefulness, and not the negativity. This will help you to maintain your ability to self-improve and know when you have genuinely done something wrong, without letting you fall into the trap of criticising everything that you do.

Tip Four: Take Up New Hobbies

When you are feeling particularly low, you may find that you lose interest in many things that you used to enjoy. Sometimes, taking up something new will help you to rekindle your passion and reignite your interest in life.

You could try asking around your friend group to see what hobbies are common if you are stuck for ideas. There are so many different hobbies, and if you have lost your current interests, you might be really struggling to think of something else that sounds appealing.

It may take a while to discover something new that you enjoy, but if you keep going, you might find your spark in the oddest place. Consider doing something completely different to your normal interests, and see how it goes.

For example, if you are a keen painter or artist, you might want to try climbing or playing a sport. If you enjoy gaming, take up a pottery class. You could try jewellery making, photography, drumming, knitting, writing, dancing, or any number of other things. Choosing something that is well outside your usual go-to options will help to avoid negative associations that you might have if you are struggling with your mood and anxiety.

Tip Five: Sleep Well

As well as exercising well, making sure that you sleep properly is a good idea. We all know that being sleep deprived can be massively detrimental in terms of mood, so establishing a good routine around sleep is one of the best ways to minimise anxiety and negativity.

If you are struggling with getting to sleep because of anxiety, this might feel like a very frustrating suggestion, because you may find that your brain won't turn off. You may want to talk to your doctor about the possibility of medication, but there are a few things you can do to help yourself relax. These all come under the umbrella term of sleep hygiene.

Firstly, establish a good sleeping routine. Aim to wake up and fall asleep at approximately the same time every day, whether it is during the week or at weekends. Don't sleep in really late at weekends (although a little lie in is fine!) and don't stay up too late either.

This lets your body clock know when it should start to activate sleep hormones and it should hopefully help you to fall asleep at the appropriate time.

Next, it is a good idea to keep all work and play items out of the bedroom, and just use it for sleeping. This will help to send cues to your brain, telling you that when you are in that room, you are there to sleep.

Avoid working on or in your bed, and keep all screens such as phones and laptops away from the bedroom. You might also find that it helps to instigate a screen ban after a certain time.

You should make your room nice and dark once you are ready to sleep, but also consider dimming the lights before you are ready to go to sleep. This helps to simulate the sun going down and will send signals to your brain to start slowing down. Swap to mood lights or a dimmable lamp before you get into bed.

If you find that you can't sleep and you aren't getting drowsy after about half an hour of trying, you should get up and do something else for a while. Some people find that yoga is calming, or you might want to read for a bit. This sort of thing helps to reset the brain and makes it easier to nod off again.

Finally, try not to eat too late at night. While it's easy to fall into the trap of a late supper or midnight snacks, this isn't good for helping yourself fall asleep. Instead, eat reasonably early and just have a drink of water before bed. This ensures you aren't sleeping on a full stomach, which can be uncomfortable and may keep you awake. If you do need a snack, have something light and easy to eat, and only have enough so that you stop feeling hungry.

Tip Six: Practice Some Meditation

Anxiety is not easy to tackle, and meditation certainly isn't a fix-all solution, but many people find that meditating can help them overcome panic attacks and bring their overall anxiety down, especially when combined with some of the other techniques offered here.

There are many videos that you can follow on YouTube to help yourself learn to meditate. You could also discuss meditation techniques with your doctor, or join a local group and learn to meditate with others.

Finding a sense of calm is a wonderful way to make yourself more resilient to storms and capable of dealing with hardships when they arise. It will bring you more confidence in yourself and who you are.

Tip Seven: Set Micro-goals

You can tackle negativity and feelings of hopelessness by proving your own ability to yourself – and the best way to do this is to achieve things.

That might sound daunting if you are feeling really down about yourself and about life. Some days, even simple tasks like getting up, washing dishes, or putting on laundry can feel overwhelming, and you might find that you just can't cope even with the idea.

On the better days, however, you should aim to set yourself some simple goals that you can easily achieve. Opt for ones that will improve your life directly, like tidying up your home, cleaning things, gardening, and doing chores. Filling in paperwork is another good one.

It's really important to be careful when you are setting mini goals for yourself. If you set too many, you may find that you get overwhelmed and can't do anything, which will then make you feel annoyed with yourself and worse about your ability to achieve things.

Instead, choose up to five goals, and prioritise carefully. Set one or two important but manageable goals, and then up to another three unimportant goals that you can do if you feel great about things.

You need to gear your goals to your own situation and your capabilities, and bear in mind that this may go up or down on any given day. For example, when you are going through a bad patch, you might find that your important goal is simply to fill in some paperwork or tidy up the kitchen. On a good day, you might tackle joining a new gym, attending a job interview, going shopping, etc.

Gearing your goals to meet your current mental state is very crucial, and you need to respect your boundaries. Do not set goals that you know you won't be able to achieve. You will end up worsening your mental state by proving to yourself that you can't do things. Make sure you do the opposite of this, by proving you can do things and getting through your goals!

CHAPTER FIVE

Accepting Sadness

Next, we are going to talk about how to accept sorrow as a part of your life. This might sound a strange one after everything we have discussed about how sadness can destroy your ability to cope and make you negative about everything, but it is important to consider.

Do you think that you can live your life totally free from sadness, and always feel good about everything?

Most people would say no. We recognise that sadness is an intrinsic part of life that we must deal with, and yet whenever it occurs, we reject it. It does not feel good, so we try to push it away or feel angry with ourselves for experiencing the emotion.

This needs to stop, because sometimes you are going to feel sad, and that is fine. You shouldn't be berating yourself when it happens, even if it appears to be without a good reason. If your mood is low, take some time to be kind to yourself and accept that your emotions will fluctuate just like the weather does. Sometimes, you have to feel sad.

Being accepting of the emotion, strangely, can make it far less intense and difficult to deal with. If you are able to welcome it as a natural but temporary part of your life, you will likely find that it passes away much more quickly than if you try to shut it out, shut it down, or pretend it doesn't exist.

Sometimes, a good cry helps. It releases oxytocin and endogenous opioids, which counteract the sadness and make both physical and emotional pain milder. If you have ever sat and watched a sad movie and felt the pleasantness of crying during it, you'll know how the release works.

Don't bottle tears up when you feel like they would help. Crying and being in touch with the emotions prevents them from taking over your life, giving them a release and 'letting it out.'

You don't have to cry to recognise and express emotions, either. You just have to respect what you are feeling and not try to suppress it. When something bothers you, acknowledge – both to yourself and to others if possible – that it is not okay, and think about why.

Many people feel that they have to push down their emotions and put a brave face on things, but doing this is a recipe for disaster in many cases. It is much better to let people know when you need support.

Being able to do this is not something that happens overnight. If you are struggling with your emotions, you are going to have to spend weeks working towards acceptance of them. When you find yourself blocking out and suppressing sadness, you need to consciously change your approach.

One of the best ways to do this is verbally affirming to yourself that it is okay to be sad. Tell yourself this in whatever phrasing feels most natural to you, and repeat it to yourself whenever you need to. It is okay to feel sad. Sadness is as natural and necessary as rain. It is as important to our growth and well-being as water is to plants. It may be unpleasant while it lasts, but it will help us.

Welcome sadness. Get in touch with your emotions by reading sad books or watching sad movies, and let yourself feel the full weight of them. Sometimes, it's easier to deal with the sorrow instigated by something fictional, and this can help you build up to handling real life sorrow more effectively.

Being in touch with your emotions does not mean that you wallow in sadness at all times – because that's no more healthy for you than persistent flooding is for plants. It means that you accept the storms, the bad days, the anxiety, and you give them a place in your life, but a limited place. They are not permitted to drown out everything else, but they are permitted to exist, and respected in their existence.

This may make it easier to be kind to yourself, because you won't add anger to already negative feelings. You won't mentally rant at yourself for feeling low, or feel guilty or frustrated on top of anxiety. Instead, you will realise that these things are an aspect of life, they have their place, and you are in control.

Accepting your emotions empowers you to deal with them better, and that is essential. Sadness belongs in our lives, and we can handle it better if we don't try to shut it out entirely. Balance is crucial, and you need both sadness and happiness to achieve it.

CHAPTER SIX

Mental And Physical Decluttering

One of the things that often adds to anxiety is the amount of clutter that most people accumulate both mentally and physically. When your space is cluttered, your stress levels naturally rise, because you are aware of all these 'things' that need dealing with, and you don't have the scope to think clearly or act decisively.

Physical Decluttering

We're going to look at physical clutter first.

Clutter adds to your physical workload, because it takes far longer to clean a cluttered space than it does to clean an empty one. If you have to spend an hour tidying up before you can start wiping down surfaces and dusting corners, you are going to find it much harder to keep on top of things like housework.

You are probably already aware of how physical clutter adds to anxiety. If you have ever glanced surreptitiously at a pile of laundry or a stack of dirty dishes in the sink, you will know that slight feeling of dread as you try not to acknowledge a task that hasn't been done and needs to be addressed.

You might also know full well just how good it feels to get an anxiety-inducing task out of the way and finished, especially if it has been hanging over you for a long time. Often, doing the task is not nearly as bad as the buildup to doing the task seems. Many people find this with taxes, work paperwork, assignments, etc. The interim period between the task being set and being completed, in which you are very aware of the 'needs to be done' looming ever-closer, is the hardest part.

This sort of thing drains your mental energy, even if it's just a case of 'I need to tidy up the bookcase later.' There might be minimal stress associated with it, but there is a sense of pressure, a feeling of 'should do X,' and this can be very wearing. It takes up energy just to think and plan and organise like this, so even minor tasks like tidying a part of a room or doing the dishes can be exhausting.

Clutter makes everything worse because, of course, things need tidying up very much more frequently when they are cluttered. If you find that you are constantly going through kitchen drawers because you can't find the right spoon in the mess of other spoons, or you're always having to reorganise your wardrobe because the clothes don't really fit there properly, your life will be more stressful and difficult than it would be without the clutter.

Physical clutter has both a physical impact, in that you spend more time tidying up, and a mental impact, in that you have to constantly dedicate some of your brainpower to assessing and dealing with this clutter. Cutting down on the 'stuff' in your life is important, so let's look at some exercises that will help you do this.

Exercise: Physical Decluttering

Step One) Pick A Drawer

The last thing you need is to start trying to declutter your whole home at once. Choose one room to focus on, and then break it down even further by starting with a single drawer or cupboard. It is not a good idea to pull everything out at once and make a huge mess; you're likely to get absolutely overwhelmed and have to put it all back, or leave it in a heap on the floor.

Step Two) Empty The Drawer

Clear a space and tip everything out of the drawer and onto the floor or a table. Don't leave things in the drawer because they belong there, or you aren't sorting properly; empty the entire drawer. This changes your approach and ensures you are really thinking about every single thing.

Next, get three cardboard boxes – one for keep, one for donate and/or sell, and one for throwing away. Begin going through the things you own, distributing them into these three boxes.

You may find that you need more than three categories, and that's fine: do whatever works for you. Just make sure you are slowly whittling down the pile until everything is in boxes.

Step Three) Replace Things That Belong In The Drawer

Once the items have been sorted, decide what items in the 'keep' box belong in the drawer that you just emptied. Put them back, arranging them so that they will stay tidier.

Step Four) Deal With The Boxes

Next, deal with the boxes. Depending on how much you have filled them, you may want to put your donate/sell box to one side so you can add to it (making a donation trip more worthwhile), but you should get rid of your rubbish box promptly. You don't need it, and leaving it lying around will make your space feel more cluttered.

Step Five) Enjoy The Feeling

Before you move on to the next drawer, cupboard, shelf, etc., take a bit of time to appreciate your effort and achievement. Admire the newly organised space, and applaud yourself for taking the time to clear up. Praise yourself – remember, we talked about how powerful negative language is, so use some positivity here

Tip: Some people find it helps to take before and after pictures, so you can see what a difference you have made and remind yourself of your hard work.

Step Six) Carry On Decluttering

When you are ready, move on to the next space. You don't have to rush to do this, however. Don't try to tackle entire rooms in a day, but go slowly and take your time. Decluttering can be quite exhausting, especially if you are reluctant to let go of things so be patient with yourself. Rome wasn't built in a day!

Tip: If you are finding it hard to decide whether to donate/sell something, put it in the box anyway. You can take it out at a later date. If you are really unsure, put the box somewhere and keep it for six months. If you haven't missed the item by the end of this time period, it can go!

You should now have an idea about how to get on top of existing clutter. When your home is feeling a bit more spacious, make an effort to stay on top of clutter that is entering the home. Always ask yourself whether you need a new X before you buy something, and don't be afraid to quietly re-gift or donate unwanted presents. While it might feel harsh and you should be careful not to offend the gift-giver, you aren't obliged to have items you don't want and won't use in your home.

Mental Decluttering

In case you haven't already guessed, mental clutter can be quite a lot harder to deal with. It isn't nearly as easy to pinpoint, and it can be a lot more difficult to offload it when necessary. However, when you are feeling anxious or stressed, it's absolutely vital to do this. Mental clutter will exacerbate your stress immensely.

Mental clutter can take many forms, so you might find it useful to run through a few of the below categories and see which ones you feel 'speak' to you. We will then do some exercises that may help you to deal with them. Mental clutter might be:

Past Trauma

If you have dealt with difficult things in your past, you might be carrying mental clutter as a result of this. PTSD is obviously a particularly severe instance of this, but even if you don't have a mental disorder as a result of trauma, you are likely still carrying some mental weight from it.

You should talk to a licensed therapist if this is the case. Trauma needs to be addressed, and reaching out will give you the strategies to start overcoming this kind of challenge.

Regrets About The Past

Thoughts of the past can haunt us all. A sense of what will never be can become very strong when you are unhappy or feeling low, and you might spend a lot of time thinking about the 'mistakes' that you have made. Perhaps you wish you had taken different courses, gone or not gone to university, broken up or stayed in a relationship, travelled more or less, or anything else.

Regrets can be exhausting, because there is nothing concrete you can do, and they colour every aspect of daily life.

Too Many Commitments

Mental clutter isn't always about the 'heavy' stuff. It can be about the simple, everyday tasks just getting too much for you to handle. If you are juggling too many things – and so many people are – it's very easy to feel stressed and overwhelmed.

Worries About The Future

Worrying about the future is exhausting even if you aren't already feeling negative and anxious. There is such a broad range of things that could happen, it's overwhelming to start thinking about. Whether your worries are focused on loved ones, money, the economy, politics, or other facets of life, worrying excessively about the future can send your anxiety and negativity through the roof.

General Irritation

When our moods are low, most of us tend to be irritable with those around us. We don't mean to be, but when we feel bad, we project this onto others, and this can become habitual. This is bad for many reasons, bringing down everyone's moods, but it is also immensely mentally draining and can leave you feeling exhausted.

Being overly critical and grumbling about things constantly is tiring, and if it's a habit you have got into, it's one you need to find ways to break.

Seeking Perfection

Extreme expectations, for yourself and for others, is another element of mental clutter that can sap your energy. If you are always looking for things that are wrong and you can never feel pleased with anything, you will wear yourself out.

This sort of thing can be very background and almost unnoticeable, but it will reduce your ability to think. Whenever you undertake a project, you will be worrying about whether you are doing it well enough, and this will leave you tired and miserable. It might also make it hard to start the project – because you will fear failing – and that adds to your multiple commitments and sense of being overwhelmed by all the things that need to be done.

Exercise: Mental Decluttering

Step One) Make Some Lists

Sit down at your desk and make some lists about all the things that are worrying you, both big and small. A worry could be as minor as 'I forgot to get milk from the shops so we have to have toast for breakfast' or as big as 'I'm afraid I might lose my job.'

Write them all down so that you have a concrete list. This helps to reduce the abstractness that many worries thrive on.

Step Two) Categorise

Divide your list up according to the categories above, and any others that you can think of. You may also want to rank the items according to how big you think they are. For example, your list might look something like this:

Thought	Type Of Worry	Big Or Small	Solution Available
I'm frightened of being in a car accident again	Past trauma	Big	Therapy
I wish I had learned French in school	Regrets about the past	Small	Take a class

Thought	Type Of Worry	Big Or Small	Solution Available
I haven't finished my taxes	Too many commitments	Medium	Make a time to do it in
I haven't got enough savings set aside for house repairs	Worries about the future	Big	Start a savings account
Nobody pays attention when I talk	General irritation	Small	Have a discussion with family or adjust feelings about this
I will mess this project up	Seeking perfection	Medium	Seek outside help or affirmations, or self-affirm your ability to do the project

Your list is likely to look quite different to the one above, and you may choose to include other columns or categories, but this should help you to get a good idea of what your worries are. Remember that the size of the worry is completely dependent on you and how much it matters to you. Worrying about toast can be a big worry if it is having a big impact on you.

Step Three) Analyse Your List

Look back over your list carefully, and see whether any particular category is very common for you. Do you mostly worry about the future? Are day to day tasks stressing you out? Are you having difficulty balancing your commitments?

Knowing which area(s) are particularly bad for causing mental clutter can help you highlight where you need to do some work and shed some weight. Below, we'll explore some ideas for each category, helping you understand how to mentally declutter.

Dealing With Past Trauma

Past trauma is among the hardest kinds of mental clutter you will have to deal with. When you are struggling with your own brain to process something really difficult, there are a lot of challenges to overcome, and – depending on how severe the trauma was – you are likely to need help from a professional in order to cope properly.

It's important not to dismiss your trauma, especially if you realise it's causing or ties in with a lot of your other worries. Don't ignore it in the hopes that it will disappear or fade away. It is not going to.

Start to address trauma by recognising and respecting your emotions. Something horrible happened, and you owe yourself kindness and consideration. Talk to your GP about counselling or other help; there is a lot of assistance available, and you need to tap into this to help yourself offload some of this mental clutter.

Dealing With Regrets About The Past

If you find yourself thinking longingly about the past and wishing you had done something differently, take a few moments to make a list of every good thing in your life. Who do you love and care about? What do you have that you value? What experiences have shaped you?

Now, consider how many of these might not be yours if you had made different decisions. If you had dated a different person, would you still have your children? If you had not gone to college when you did, would you have met your best friend? If you had learned French in school, would you have missed out on something else?

You may be familiar with the butterfly effect, the idea that a tiny action can totally alter the course of your future. Even seemingly disconnected events can be tied together. Have a go at tying seemingly unrelated events together – this can actually be a really fun activity. Start with a decision you regret, and try to link in as many positive outcomes that it may have had as you can, even if these are a long way down the line.

For example:

I got into a relationship too young and dated a girl in school who treated me badly. It had a major knock-on effect on my self-esteem, and made it hard to date for a while. I regret that I didn't break up with her sooner, before she could have such an impact on me, because I still struggle to feel confident with dating today. However, her rejection led to a close friendship with another guy who stuck up for me, and he introduced me to his boss, who gave me a great job.

Alternatively:

I didn't pay enough attention at college, and I didn't get the grades I wanted. I dropped out, and I've never gone back. I wish I had finished my education, because it would have let me get a better job. On the other hand, I learned some good lessons about dedication that have helped me stick through a tough work situation and kept me going when my mother was ill.

You may not always feel that the 'payoff' for the bad thing was worth the loss, but looking at life events within a broad context can help to put them into perspective and show you that even when you lose, you usually win something. The win might not be great, but you should still acknowledge it.

This can really help to counteract your sense of negativity about the past, or at least give you a new view of how sometimes, something bad leads to something good. Of course, sometimes you may not know that you have 'dodged a bullet' with a choice that seems wrong in retrospect. Dropping out of college might have saved your life, and you will never even know it!

The consequences of our actions are so far reaching and small actions have such a massive impact on everything else that it is impossible to truly weigh up what was and was not a good decision. Knowing this may help to mitigate your regret about the course your life has taken, at least to a degree.

Another good strategy is to focus on the now, and get yourself engaged in new things. If you are busy thinking about the past a lot, it is probably because you are unhappy with something in your present. Find ways to change this, instead of yearning for a chance to redo.

Dealing With Too Many Commitments

If you have a lot of commitments going on, your worries are probably all focused on the things that you haven't got around to yet. These might seem petty things, but they are all adding to your mental clutter and stopping you from thinking clearly.

The worst part is, when your anxiety is high, you can't do the very thing that would solve this problem – dealing with the tasks. You will often find that you are too wired and too stressed to handle things properly, and you might not know where to start.

The best thing to do is to find a way to organise the commitments. You may then find that there are some you can drop, but even if you can't, this will help.

Some people prefer a pen and paper for organising, while others prefer apps or computer programs. Experiment and see what suits you best.

You should start by dividing your commitments up into categories, such as 'kids,' 'me,' 'partner,' 'family,' 'social,' etc. You might have a 'Christmas' category, a 'household jobs' category, a 'repairs' category, a 'paperwork' category, and so on. This may help you to make sense of some of the mental clutter.

Think of this a bit like dealing with paperwork. If you don't file your paperwork in a system that works for you, it's easy to miss important things like appointments, or lose things that you need. Categorising means that you can focus on something and deal with it at the appropriate time.

Once you have your categories, use them to make notes about the things that you need to do. For example, you might end up with something like this:

Household Jobs	Paperwork	Christmas	Other
Paint the gate	Fill in taxes	Buy gift for sister	Attend parents' evening

Household Jobs	Paperwork	Christmas	Other
Repair the steps	Request papers from doctor	Get a tree	Start a night class
Get a quote for plumbing repairs		Find out numbers for Christmas dinner	
Tidy up the sitting room			

You can then use a highlighter or numbering system to organise the jobs by priority, or add dates by which things need to be achieved.

This should remove the clutter from your head, getting it all onto paper and giving you a clear plan for moving forward. Once this has been done, stop, take a break, and de-stress before you try to move forward with anything.

Next, review your list and see if you are happy with your prioritisation. Look for tasks that can be delegated, or commitments that you can drop. Many people find it hard to say 'no' when there is a lot to do, but it is a powerful tool that will help you enormously, and sometimes, for the sake of your own mental health, you have to.

Be prepared to claim back a bit of time for yourself and guard this well. It is crucial to feeling positive. Look after and value yourself as much as you value others, and you will find you are more mentally resilient.

If you are happy with everything, start tackling the jobs a bit at a time, and don't get bogged down in too many. Set realistic goals, cross things off so that you have a sense of 'moving forward,' and work steadily until you feel you are on top of your tasks again.

Dealing With Worries About The Future

Worrying about the future often happens late at night, when you are tired and there is nothing you can do about it. If this sort of worrying is increasing your anxiety and stress levels and making you feel negative, it's probably also robbing you of sleep – which will, in turn, make you feel considerably more anxious.

Take action during the day, when you are clear-headed. You might feel like this is a waste of time if the worries mostly bother you at night, but doing so may help to improve your sleep and your overall mood.

Use your list from the first exercise to identify exactly what worries you about the future, and then decide if this is something that you can take action on. Usually, there will be something you can do, even if it does not get rid of the risk entirely.

For example, if you are worried about your health, you can start exercising and eating healthily, and this may help to mitigate the fear. If you are worried about finances, look at insurance options, set up a savings plan, etc.

Some worries are hard to mitigate, because they are too abstract to deal with, but you can at least address the concrete ones. This should give you a sense of empowerment. Often, worrying about the future results in a sense of helplessness, and taking action to mitigate your worries will reduce them, even if it does not completely get rid of them.

Don't ignore worries about the future. Discuss them with your partner or with friends and family, and make plans that will help you to feel safe. While you can't avert (or even predict) every crisis, this should reduce your sense of stress.

Dealing With General Irritation

As we mentioned, it's easy to fall into the habit of feeling generally irritated by life. You might find that you snap at loved ones and yourself, that little things are unnecessarily troublesome, and that everything feels difficult.

The first step for dealing with this problem is to become conscious of the issue. Make yourself aware of your language and attitude, especially towards the people you love. You might be unintentionally hurting someone very dear to you just because we depend upon habits, and irritation can become a habit when you are feeling negative.

Talk to people about your attitude, and how they feel about it. Ask them to pinpoint behaviour that upsets them, and make notes about what you feel needs to be improved and how you can improve. Be aware that breaking habits is very hard, and cut yourself some slack when it doesn't go well. As long as you keep trying, it will get better.

Often, replacing a bad habit with a good one is easier than just getting rid of the bad habit. If you find that you swear when you spill a drink (remember, language is powerful!), try replacing the cursing with an amusing phrase that makes you smile.

If you snap at your partner, friends, or children, make yourself pause before interacting, and then find a gentler way to say what you wish to express. Consciously moderate your tone of voice.

Next, make a habit of saying nice things to people. Think about how much you appreciate them, and what you love about them, and then verbalise these things. Why do your family matter to you? What do they do well?

Make a list of the ways in which you feel you can build the confidence of those around you, and use them at every opportunity. Pay compliments to others and to yourself. Tell others when you feel you have done something well. Appreciate the things around you.

Even something like 'the sky is beautiful today' can boost your mood. You don't have to feel it very strongly to say it, and saying it will make you feel better. Equally, 'thank you for washing up,' or 'wow, what a clever idea' can give your partner a feel-good boost, and make you feel better yourself.

Fight negativity with positivity and don't let irritation become a habit, or you will wear yourself and your family down!

Dealing With Seeking Perfection

If you are stressed because nothing ever seems 'right' enough to you, there are also steps you can take. This desire to be perfect is a definite cause of anxiety and may make it very difficult for you to do things, which adds to other kinds of stress, so it needs to be dealt with.

Fortunately, there are a few different strategies you can implement.

Firstly, use the power of language. When you make a comment on something you have done, always say something positive. You can follow this up with 'but X could be better' if you choose, but always say something good about it. Tell others what you think went well and why you are pleased.

Next, seek positive affirmation from others and genuinely listen to it. If your boss tells you that you did well at something, believe them, and use this compliment to fuel your sense of confidence. The same goes for when your partner or a friend praises you.

Remember, we are often our own worst critics, and if you are too harsh and never satisfied with your own work, you won't get anything done!

As another strategy, set a timer for yourself, and remember that life is short. In most cases, perfect does not matter. What matters is 'done.' You could spend your whole life perfecting the paint in the bathroom, but you don't need to – you can do other things instead.

Learn to be satisfied with 'good' and to value 'good enough' as a truly important concept. Perfection might be nice in some instances, but often 'good enough' is actually better, because it means you have used your time well.

This is not to say that you should take no pride in your work and always do the bare minimum, but you need to recognise when your achievements are sufficient for the situation, and feel satisfied with them.

Take pictures of 'before and after' moments, and review them to remind yourself just how much you have done. Make albums of your proudest achievements. Appreciate your work. You don't have to be boastful to feel proud of the things you do, and reminding yourself that you are skilled and talented can help to dissolve the need for perfection, and make you satisfied with 'good.'

CHAPTER SEVEN

Dealing With The Hard Days

Another important aspect of eliminating negativity is the hard days, and how you handle these. Start this chapter by taking some time to think about how you deal with a difficult day, and answer some of the questions below.

What do you do when you first realise you are having a hard day?

What are the five top signs you are having a hard day?

Do you tell your family/colleagues when you are having a hard day?

Do you think about your day in context? Was yesterday a hard day too? Do you think tomorrow will be? Are you tra'pping yourself in a cycle of negativity or are you aware that the difficulties will pass?

Next, try some of the following steps.

1) Keep a 'hard day' diary and write down a success or two that you have during the day. This does not need to be a big success, but anything you feel went well.

Doing this helps to dispel the illusion that the day has been a complete write-off and nothing has worked. Many people feel that the day has been wasted when things go wrong, and a diary of your achievements can help with this problem.

2) Choose some easy tasks for yourself. This method ties in with the mini goals we discussed above, but it involves more actively planning your day around your mood. If you have woken up and you aren't feeling good, see if any of your more challenging tasks can be swapped to another day. Obviously, some things have immovable deadlines, but make yourself some breathing space if possible.

This is an act of self-care that says you are going to deal with things when you can, but recognises you aren't currently fit to do so. Taking this attitude and sense of responsibility when it comes to your well-being is crucial, and conveys respect to your feelings.

3) Drink some water and eat something. Our moods are often far more connected with our physical well-being than we think. If you have not recently eaten or drunk anything, have a snack and some water. You may not feel better immediately, but this is a good way to ensure your body has the fuel it needs to cope with the day.

4) Create a gratitude list. Sit down for a few minutes and write out the things that you are grateful for. This may be anything from a beautiful sunset to your best friend or your pet. Put this list somewhere that you can see it, and use it whenever you need a pick me up.

You should try to add some things to it that are directly positive about you. You might be grateful for your kindness or your resilience or your intelligence or even just something like your hair. It can be very hard to feel positive about yourself on a bad day, so take opportunities on the good days to build up this list and make it more comprehensive.

5) Make a 'good things' jar. Similar to the gratitude list, you can make a jar of good things that have happened. These can be as big or as small as you like, but they are a great way to break up the flow of negativity and the sense that you aren't moving forward or enjoying positive events. Write them on slips of paper and add them to a jar or box. When you feel down, take these out and use them to drive your sense of positivity.

6) Have a shower and do some exercise. Depending on how bad your anxiety and negative thinking is, you might feel that this is beyond you. That's fine if so, but if you are able to, have a shower and/or do a bit of exercise. We discussed the importance of exercise and the endorphins it releases, and even some gentle yoga can help.

Taking a shower or having a long, hot soak in the bath often makes you feel better too, and you can add to this with fresh bedding and clean, comfy clothing. Spoil yourself with nice soaps or a new shampoo, and then relax for a while and put all the things that you need to do aside.

7) Get outside into nature. Make use of local green spaces if possible, and get yourself out of the house. Many people who work from home find that they suffer from cabin fever and a sense of repetitiveness that can lead to lethargy simply because they are always in the same place day after day.

Walking in nature has been proven to boost your mood. If you don't have anywhere local to walk, try doing a bit of gardening, as this also improves your mood. Even looking after houseplants can help if you don't have access to any outdoor space.

8) Chat to a friend. If you're feeling stuck in your own head, reach out to someone. You don't have to tell them that you're feeling down if this is too hard, but make contact and talk. A reminder that the world exists outside the negativity in your head can help.

If you feel capable of doing so, talk to your friend about what's making you down. They may be able to think of some solutions, offer reassurance, or just generally make you feel better. Don't be afraid to reach out!

9) Watch or read something uplifting. Getting out of your own head for a bit is a good way to change your feelings about the world and reduce the intensity of anxiety. A book is a great way to get yourself focused on another world, but if that feels daunting, a movie or even just a TV show is a great alternative.

Pick something that is engaging, even if it isn't necessarily mood-boosting. Often, all you need is to just think about something else for a while, and when you come back to 'your world,' things will seem much less overwhelming.

10) Listen to music. Good music is a proven way to change your mood. Choose some upbeat tunes and dance around to them – the movement will release endorphins, and the music will lift your mood. You could even make a playlist of your top mood lifting songs and keep it handy for the days when you're struggling. Add to this whenever you find a new tune that you particularly enjoy.

11) Try adult colouring. Many people have found that adult colouring books are a great way to help themselves relax. Colouring is good for engaging your brain and keeping you from stressing out about things, but it's a low stakes activity that doesn't have any impact if it goes wrong.

12) Do some baking or play an instrument. Again, selecting activities that are engaging and have a point, but don't matter if they go wrong will help to attack negativity and stress. They give you something to focus on and think about, but there is no massive loss if something goes awry. You can just have a go another day. Baking does result in the loss of ingredients, but if you choose simple recipes, you'll get a nice treat that you can enjoy to reward yourself for your work. Some people find cooking relaxing, but if this doesn't work for you, look for a similar activity that is soothing and mentally stimulating.

Employ any or all of these strategies, and search for combinations that work for you. You do not need to use everything on this list to help yourself handle a bad day; just try out the different techniques and find some that work. Everybody responds to stress in different ways, and likewise, different solutions work for different people.

You may even find that on different days, different techniques work. Depending on how bad the anxiety is, some days you may have to just settle for doing nothing and accept it, whereas on other days, you may find you can get a few things done and make yourself feel better as a result.

It is a good idea to keep a record of your bad days, and track your mood. You can use a simple diary for this, and flick through any time to see how things are going. This might help you to know when it's time to talk to a doctor or take more serious action. We'll cover mood diaries in more detail later.

CHAPTER EIGHT

Self Love

Self love is one of the most powerful tools you can use against anxiety and negativity. We have already explored how negativity often gets turned inwards and affects us intensely when we are feeling low. You can fight this negativity with self love, but it takes a lot of work. We're going to look at some top techniques for self love.

Language

In Chapter Four, we talked about mood boosting activities and positive language, but we're going to recap a bit on this here, because the language you use in your everyday life and about yourself is extremely important.

If you followed the exercises in that chapter, you should already have begun to pick up on some of the negative things you say about yourself, and altered them towards more positive statements. Now, however, it's time to think about taking this technique further.

We are enormously swayed by the words that we hear regularly, and your opinion of yourself will be massively altered by how you talk about yourself and how others talk about you. By building positivity into your language, you will find that you boost your sense of self love over time.

Let's look at how you can do this.

Exercise: Loving Language

Start to make a habit out of using self-appreciative language. You may want to begin by doing this in your head, as it often feels quite odd at first.

Take a simple activity and tell yourself that you did well at it. This can be the simplest activity in the world, and it might seem a bit silly, but praise yourself anyway. You made that sandwich brilliantly well. You have swept the floor like a pro. You are dressed like a king or queen. You rock at making a cup of coffee.

Keep doing this at every opportunity, and do it about other people too, even if you choose not to verbalise it. Praise everyone and everything so that you reprogramme your mental approach to the world, other people, and – most importantly – yourself.

You can couple this with praising yourself aloud when you start to get more confident. You don't have to do this excessively; just saying 'I'm really pleased with how well I've done this,' or 'I think this went well,' can be enough to boost your mood and opinion of yourself.

It's important to do this even when you don't feel like it and you aren't happy. That doesn't mean you have to be insincere, but you should always try and find some value in what you have done. It's rare that your input will be worse than no input at all, so if you have done anything, it will be better than it was. Try to feel pleased with that and pick at least one aspect that you feel you have done well with.

If nothing else, you will have learned how to do it better next time, or identified mistakes that you should avoid in future. Whenever you complete an activity, review your progress with a positive bias, and admire yourself for what you have achieved.

Boundaries

One of the most important aspects of loving yourself is respecting yourself, and doing that means respecting your limits. Many people shrink in on themselves for the sake of other people's comfort and this has the unfortunate side effect of telling yourself that you are less valuable than others.

If, for example, a room is too warm, but you don't open the window because others might be cold, you are sending an implicit message that the comfort of others takes priority over your own comfort.

Sometimes, this will be necessary; we can't always put our own comfort before that of other people. However, if you are always shrinking down to make more space for others, you are more likely to stop valuing your feelings even when they don't affect anyone else's.

Instead, you need to recognise what makes you comfortable and happy, and implement some boundaries that help with this. Once these boundaries have been set, you should respect them, and only break them when you consciously decide they need to be broken because of extreme circumstances.

Other people may not appreciate boundaries that you set, especially if you are dealing with toxic or negative people. They will see your boundaries as an attack on them, and may respond by trying to break the boundaries down or ignoring them. It is important to recognise and deal with this sort of behaviour, but let's first discuss how to set the boundaries.

Exercise: Setting Boundaries

Start by making a list of the things that make you uncomfortable. As always, these don't have to be huge issues to be significant. They can be quite minor things, like someone taking advantage of your time or not respecting your space.

For example, if you share a house, it may be that your housemate enters your room without permission and this makes you feel uncomfortable. Ignoring this is a way of telling yourself that your feelings don't matter as much as your housemate's convenience, and it should not be done.

Instead, recognise the issue, write it down, and then decide what action you are going to take to convey the new boundary. Usually, this will involve talking to the person that is breaking the boundary and expressing that you aren't okay with it.

You may find that it helps to start with something small, as many people find this an extremely daunting task. Choose a person you feel reasonably comfortable with, select a boundary that you wish to set, and decide how you are going to tell them about it.

It's a good idea to explain your feelings as you do this. For example, you might say to someone 'It makes me feel rushed when you visit unexpectedly. Please can you let me know before you drop round?'

If even that feels too big for you, find something smaller. Ask someone not to borrow your things, or not to text you early in the morning. Find something that helps you to grow, own your space, and establish boundaries that others can use to guide themselves and moderate how they behave in relation to you.

You may find yourself feeling guilty when you first start to do this, so make sure you remind yourself that you are as worthy of consideration as any other person. Would you mind if someone else asked you for the same consideration? If not, there is no reason that they should mind you asking.

Exercise: Making Sure Boundaries Are Respected

This is much more difficult, but sometimes you will find that people do not respect the boundaries you set. This may be because they don't respect you, or because they subconsciously aren't taking you seriously or don't realise that you mean it.

Sometimes, it will just be a case of them needing time to adjust to the new rule and forgetting it occasionally. You should be accepting of this; it often takes time to adjust and people don't always mean to disrespect you just because they have failed to do something you have asked.

However, if it keeps happening, you will need to firm up the boundary. Firstly, do this by reiterating it exists at least once, possibly more (depending on the relationship that you have with them). Explain to them why it is important to you.

If the person is still refusing to acknowledge the boundary, you will have to think about what action to take. Why are they ignoring the boundary? Is there a good reason? Are they simply not taking you seriously?

Assess the boundary and decide if it is reasonable and important to you. Do not just ignore it because it's easier than allowing conflict to arise; your boundaries are key, and if you don't respect them, others won't, and you may end up resenting both the other party and yourself.

If the boundary is reasonable, you need to sit and have a conversation with the other person about why they are refusing to acknowledge it. Find out what it is that stops them from listening, and what it would take to get them to listen. It is okay to compromise if you can find a new route forwards, but don't give up on your need for rules and don't let them take your concessions for granted.

If a person still will not respect the boundaries that you set (whether or not they say that they will, the actions are what matter), you need to remove them from your life. You may have to cut them off entirely, or you might find that you can revoke their rights to do certain things in your life.

A few practical steps you can take, depending on the action that is crossing the boundary, include:

☐ Not answering your phone

☐ Installing a lock on your door

☐ Only responding to messages at certain times

☐ Not visiting spaces where you are uncomfortable

☐ Denying them access to your home

☐ Not agreeing to favours that are asked of you

☐ Refusing to loan money

☐ Not engaging in certain conversation topics (e.g. politics) at all

You might feel guilty about establishing boundaries like this, but doing so is healthy for both you and for others. It lets others know that they are allowed to set similar boundaries themselves, and normalises doing so. It shows that you respect yourself and encourages others to do the same. It can be hard to stick to your guns when people consistently ignore your boundaries, but make sure that you do so, and don't be bullied into abandoning rules that you have set for your own comfort.

Asking Others For Help

An aspect of self love is recognising and accepting that you cannot do and be everything. No single person is good at everything, and recognising your limitations will help you. Remember, we talked about the value of accepting 'good enough,' rather than constantly striving for perfection. This is the same idea.

Part of this process involves asking others when you need help with something. Many of us find that it is hard to ask for favours because we feel we aren't worthy of them, but that's exactly why doing so can be so important. Asking for favours reminds you that you are worth the attention of others – especially when they agree.

You shouldn't take a refusal as a sign of your unworthiness, either. It may just be that the person isn't in a position to do what you asked for whatever reason – they may not have enough mental or physical energy for the task. However, if they can do it, their outlay of energy (or whatever else the favour might involve) is a clear indication of the value that they place in you.

Asking for help is another aspect of this, and it's one that many people find hard, because it means – to some degree at least – admitting your limitations. Even something as simple as asking for help with the washing up or the cleaning says 'I am not in as good a position as you are to complete this task.' Some people equate it with saying 'I am incapable of this,' and that isn't a good feeling to have.

However, humans are social animals, and we massively benefit from working together and putting group efforts into things. We thrive when we play to our strengths and allow others to do the same. There is nothing wrong with acknowledging that you can't do something, because we shouldn't expect ourselves to be good at everything. Instead, you should accept that you have weaknesses, recognise what they are, and turn to others when you need assistance.

This is also an important aspect of self care, because it gives you permission to take a break sometimes. It allows someone else to take over and handle things for a while, and that is good for both you and for them.

Exercise: Asking For Help

It takes a lot of practice to get used to asking for help. Start with something small and ask somebody you trust. Get your partner to make you a cup of tea, or to look over some paperwork for you. Get your friend to pick some milk up from the shops.

Slowly build up from there, working on asking for small favours until you feel comfortable with doing so. Once you are feeling more confident, branch out a bit. Ask for help at work. Get your friends to pitch in when you are going through a tough patch. Reach out and request assistance when you need it.

Offering Help

On the flip side of asking for help, offering help can be an enormously empowering thing that improves your confidence and opinion of yourself. When you know that you can do something, check whether someone would like help with it.

You have to couple this with a healthy respect for 'no thanks,' but if you can manage that, you will find that your offers for help are usually welcomed and highly appreciated. This will strengthen your relationships with others and make you feel like you are a useful, contributing member of the group.

You might be able to do something as simple as taking over the washing up when your partner is tired, or dropping off your friend's children at school. It doesn't have to be complicated to be useful, and it doesn't have to be a big job. That means that even if you aren't feeling great, you can offer help to others.

Sometimes, it's easier to do something for someone else than it is to do it for ourselves. Helping another person doesn't always directly contribute to a sense of self love, but it can give you a boost. Overall, helping others does make us feel better about ourselves and who we are, so if you can find it in yourself to do something for someone else when you are feeling negative, do so. It might just turn your whole mood around.

This can also help to counteract the sense of 'everything is bad,' which many of us start to feel when we are in a negative mood. By proving to yourself that kindness and selflessness are part of everyday life, you can make the world feel just a bit brighter, and be an integral part of this brightness.

Exercise: Offering Help

Once again, starting small is often the best way to build up to offering help. Choose someone that you know well and offer to help them with something. If it's too much to take over entirely, just offer assistance. Fold the washing with your partner, or take your friend's dog for a walk. Help your children with their homework.

You might then want to start to offer to help your colleagues at work, if applicable. Don't be offended if they say no, as some people struggle to accept help, but if they say yes, give them a hand.

It's important to build up slowly; don't offer help that is beyond you, or you will potentially upset the other person, and you may feel bad about yourself. Choose small, seemingly inconsequential things to help with, and you will soon find your faith in your own abilities growing.

CHAPTER NINE

The Future Plan

What about going forward? How is life going to change?

One thing that you can be sure of is that you will still encounter difficulties. Your life is not going to become noticeably different, although it may become noticeably easier if you manage to reduce your negativity. You will still have storms to weather, and you will still have days when life seems too hard to handle.

Knowing and accepting this should make your journey easier, because you won't feel totally crushed when things go awry. It may also help you to go easy on yourself when things are hard. You won't expect too much of yourself or feel that you have to achieve perfection and always be cheerful.

You can fall back on the strategies we've discussed any time that you need them in the coming months and years. Keep using them to deal with slumps and difficult times, and to keep your overall habits positive.

Whenever you notice negativity creeping in and things getting harder, you can make use of the techniques above, but you may also find it helpful to use them at other times too. That's why we're going to cover a mood diary next.

Mood Diaries

A mood diary logs your mood over a period of time, and it can be a very useful tool in the fight against negativity and anxiety. Knowledge is power, and understanding your mood can really empower you to control it.

For example, if you know that you are always emotional after you have had a sleepless night, it becomes easier to understand and moderate your behaviour accordingly. If you know you are short tempered after travelling, you can equally make use of this knowledge and make an extra effort to keep your temper in check.

A mood diary is an ongoing tool that you can use to understand and moderate your feelings and emotions. You don't have to keep it at all times, but the more you make use of it, the more powerful and helpful it will be.

Exercise: Making A Mood Diary

Keeping a diary of your mood is one of the best ways to handle negativity and stop it from taking over your life. You should try to use a notebook that you particularly like for this. You can track your mood in whatever way feels natural to you, but you may find it useful to do something like this:

Monday	Morning	Afternoon	Evening	Events	Mood Influence	Overall
	Okay	Bad	Better	Left my lunch at home and had to buy some	Bad	7/10
				Partner made dinner	Good	
				Cleaned up living room	Good	
				Put away laundry	Neutral	

You could also score your mood out of ten for each time of day if you prefer, or colour code your mood notes. Alternatively, keep a log of events and simply highlight them in a certain colour to show how they affected your mood. Using colours is a great way to make this tool very visual and ensure you can see patterns.

The advantage of correlating events to moods is that it will help you to pinpoint any negative patterns that are having a big impact on your life. For instance, if there is a pattern of forgetting something consistently, you will have a greater chance of detecting this than if you fail to keep a log.

This empowers you to take action against negative events that are having a consistent impact on your life. While one-off events will certainly still occur, you can eliminate or at least mitigate some of the issues that you otherwise face, making changes to your habits to improve your overall quality of life.

Once you have begun keeping a mood diary, take the time to review it on a regular basis. Once a month is a good idea, if possible. Take a look at both positive influences and people, and negative influences and people, and adjust your life decisions accordingly. If you feel unhappy with the trajectory your life is taking, you can take action to change it, armed with a good understanding of what needs changing.

You should also review your mood diary every few months, so you get a bigger picture of your life and the things that influence your mood day to day. Use this information as a means of charting your course forwards, and deciding what you would like to do with your life in the long term.

Do more of the things that bring you joy, and you will find yourself much more positive about life.

Mental Resilience

Building up your mental resilience is a key part of tackling negativity in the long term. Unless you can do this, you will find that your mood massively fluctuates and small problems knock you off course.

Resilience is often described as the ability to withstand blows or being put under pressure. It can also refer to an object being flexible and having the ability to return to its previous state when it has withstood external pressure. The phrase refers to your capacity to recover quickly after an unpleasant event.

Mental resilience is crucial to weathering storms, and you need to build up your mental resilience, or you will find that every blow in life takes a long time to recover from. We need to be able to recover – since we are inevitably going to encounter things that make us suffer in life – so let's explore what mental resilience involves.

It may help to think of your mental resilience like a metre or as tokens. If you spend too much on one thing, you will have less left for another. Many of us think that we should be able to handle endless amounts of problems, and underestimate how long it can take to bounce back from a challenge.

Don't take your mental resilience for granted or expect it to stretch limitlessly. Think of it in a concrete, countable way instead – whatever makes sense to you. You only have a certain amount of it, and if you try to spread it too thinly, you will put yourself under immense pressure and leave yourself stressed, worn down, and possibly even crumbling.

Respecting when your resilience is being tested and therefore spent enables you to make better decisions about what you can and cannot cope with. For example, if you know that you are under a lot of social pressure currently – perhaps a family member is ill – you may choose not to take on a big project at work, because you will recognise that you shouldn't add more stress to your environment.

Exercise: Spending Resilience Tokens

Collect up some counters and give yourself a particular amount – say up to fifty. Next, get a large sheet of paper and draw some circles on it. Some of these will be long term or permanent challenges that you deal with, such as mental illness, poorly relatives, work stress, care commitments, or other issues.

Other circles can include short term or medium term points of stress. Examples include being on your period, dealing with a cold or other minor illness, small injuries, commitments to friends (e.g. pet sitting), work projects, etc. Note that these can be large things, even if they are going to be short lived; dealing with a death takes up a lot of mental resilience, and yet can be quite short term if the person was not close to you.

It is also important to note that mental resilience is not exclusively related to negative things. You need mental resilience to deal with anything stressful, even if it relates to a positive change. For example, having a baby takes tokens, even if the baby was planned, wanted, and is very loved. Moving house takes mental resilience.

If you use a large sheet of paper, you can keep adding circles. For short term, transient circles, you may want to write in pencil so that you can rub out and change the headings when necessary, but it's often nice to leave impactful circles in – they may keep having an influence, and you can look back on all the things that you have dedicated your energy to over the years.

Once you have your sheet of paper, decide how many tokens you should have, and start distributing them. You might decide that you need three points or more on some of the harder issues you are managing, whereas others will take only one.

By the time you have finished this exercise, you should still have a small number of mental resilience tokens to play with. These are your day to day tokens and you need these for managing minor stressors in daily life.

If you have ever felt like you are about to crumble over the tiniest thing – a dropped cup of tea or a burnt slice of toast – it may be because you have spent too many mental resilience tokens in another place, and you have none left to deal with the difficult moments.

If this happens to you, spend a bit of time reassessing your tokens, where they are, and whether you are happy with their distribution. You can gain more mental resilience tokens by putting time and effort into self care and doing things that make you happy – and therefore better able to cope with the challenges in life – but you can't get an infinite amount.

A major blow can gulp up all your mental resilience tokens and leave you feeling as though you are floundering and incapable of handling anything, so it's important to be careful. If this happens, treat yourself gently and give yourself time to recover. Allow others to help you and spend their points for you where you can, and withdraw from other commitments to conserve your energy.

Once in a while, you should review your circles so that you can remove ones that are no longer relevant and add any new ones that have come into play. How often you need to do this will heavily depend on your life and how much it changes, but it's a good idea to check in every month or two. You can redistribute your tokens accordingly and see how you are doing.

It's important to note that when you are assessing your circles, there is no time limit on the effect a circle can have. If, for example, you have 'mum's death' as a circle, you don't need to set an end date to this. It may still be affecting you years later, although you will probably find that the tokens in the circle decrease with time. It may remain on your life map forever, though. Don't feel you have to take it away just because a certain amount of time has passed.

Conclusion

You hopefully now have a good sense of why anxiety and negativity can take over your life, and how easily this can happen. If you are grappling with these things, don't worry; they are transient, and they will not last forever. In the hardest moments, reminding yourself that such times will eventually pass – even if you can't currently see a way forwards – will often help.

Whenever you start to feel negative, turn to the techniques in this book for help, but also turn to professionals if you need to. Mental health is at least as important as physical health, and it will shape the course of your life to inestimable degrees, so do not ignore it because you feel like you are being dramatic or your feelings aren't worthwhile.

The more we open up to each other about the challenges we are facing and the emotional weight that many people are struggling with, the easier it becomes to start a dialogue and help each other. Talk about your struggles, and other people will share theirs.

We can learn a great deal from each other, the challenges we face, and how we deal with them, and it's crucial to do so. Along with all the techniques in this book, make a point of opening conversations about your difficulties. When you are struggling and when you are feeling well, talk about your mental health, talk about the power of negativity, and help others and yourself strive for positivity.

Disclaimer

This book contains opinions and ideas of the author and is meant to teach the reader informative and helpful knowledge while due care should be taken by the user in the application of the information provided. The instructions and strategies are possibly not right for every reader and there is no guarantee that they work for everyone. Using this book and implementing the information/recipes therein contained is explicitly your own responsibility and risk. This work with all its contents, does not guarantee correctness, completion, quality or correctness of the provided information. Misinformation or misprints cannot be completely eliminated.

Printed in Great Britain
by Amazon